The Kindness Book

BY WELLERAN POLTARNEES

LAUGHING ELEPHANT BOOKS
2000

Fourth printing. Printed in Hong Kong.
ISBN 1-883211-02-6

Laughing Elephant Books
PO Box 4399 • Seattle
98104-0399

Preface

Books that try to teach moral lessons to children are out of favor with both readers and critics. I think that is so, not because there is anything essentially wrong with the wish to recommend a path to young minds, but rather that the teaching is too frequently ill-concealed within a story, and as a consequence we feel either that we are the intended victims of deception, or are being condescended to.

The Kindness Book is blatantly moral. It says, "The right thing to do is to be kind." I think few will be offended by it, for its purpose is clear, its method direct, and the result straightforward.

W. P.

I remember one time she pulled off her apron after two days and nights nursing a neighbor lady and said, "They ain't no feelin' in the world like takin' on somebody wilted and near bout gone, and you do what you can, and then all a-sudden the pore thang starts to put out new growth and git well."

– Olive Ann Burns

In order to be truly kind, we need to think and feel as others do. Once we understand that, we will know how best to give of our kindness.

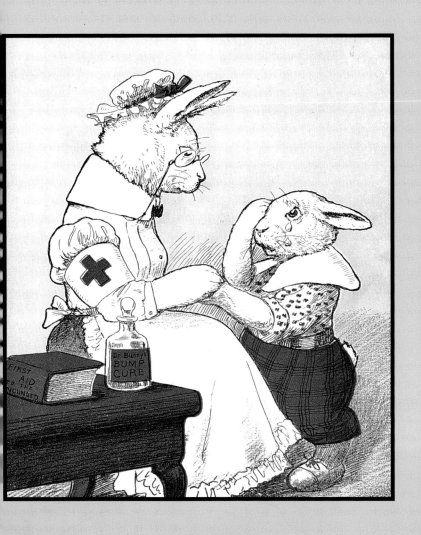

Life is made up, not of great sacrifices or duties, but of little things in which smiles and kindness and small obligations, given habitually, are what win and preserve the heart and secure comfort.
— Sir Humphrey Davy

Kindness comes in all sizes.
Sometimes it is only a little thing we give
— a trifle, a smile, a piece of fruit, a place
to rest one's head.

Let us open up our natures, throw wide the doors of our hearts and let in the sunshine of good will and kindness.

– O.S. Marden

One of the good things about kindliness is that it takes us out of the confinement of self into a larger world of many lives with many needs. When we offer what we have to give, we learn.

We may scatter the seeds of courtesy and kindness around us at so little expense. Some of them will inevitably fall on good ground, and grow up into benevolence in the minds of others; and all of them will bear the fruit of happiness in the bosom whence they spring.

— Jeremy Bentham

Visiting someone who is lonely, and bringing them some small mark of our caring, is a kindness available to us almost every day of our lives. A few minutes, a few kindly words and a smile can make a great difference to another's day.

Little deeds of kindness,
little words of love,
Help to make earth happy
like the Heaven above.
– Julia A.F. Carney

Differences of skill open wide the doors of opportunity. A great kindness can involve for us only a very small effort.

If you stop to be kind, you must swerve often from your path.

– Mary Webb

When life is at risk we have no choice of whether to be kind. We must also use our stores of strength, courage and ingenuity.

I expect to pass through this world but once. Any good therefore that I can do, or any kindness that I can show to any fellow creature, let me do it now. Let me not defer or neglect it, for I shall not pass this way again.

— Anonymous

WE NEVER WASTE TIME WHEN WE ARE HELPING OTHERS

Wise sayings often fall on barren ground, but a kind word is never thrown away.
                                                    – Arthur Helps

Those in grief are often so con-
sumed by their sorrow that they seem not
to recognize the concern of others, but
kindness is somewhere sensed, and can
only do good.

*If what must be given is given willingly
the kindness is doubled.*

– Syrus

**Kindness should be a frame of mind
in which we are alert to chances to do, to
give, to cheer.**

Life is short, and we never have too much time for gladdening the hearts of those who are travelling the dark journey with us. Oh, be swift to love, make haste to be kind!

– Henri-Frédéric Amiel

Kindness can be a duty or a great pleasure. The more we can make it the latter, the more complete it is.

Picture Credits

Front Cover
• A. J. MacGreggor. *Jeremey's Day in the Country*, circa 1950s.
Endpapers
Front & Back
• H. Willebeek Le Mair. *The Children's Corner*. 1916.
Frontispiece
• Anonymous. *Blackies Children's Annual*. circa 1925.
Title Page
• Anonymous. *Dog Tales and other Tales*. circa 1890.
Copyright Page
• Ernest Griset. *Guck! Guck!* circa 1900.
Preface Page
• Mary Baker. *The Pixies and The Silver Crown*. 1927.
Interior Pages
• J.G. Sowerby. *Afternoon Tea*. circa 1880.
• L.J. Bridgman. *Bumps & Thumps*. 1903.
• Anonymous. *Dies schöne Buch dem braven Kind*. circa 1900.
• Helena Maguire. *Nursery Land*. circa 1905.
• Anonymous. *Dies schöne Buch dem braven Kind*. circa 1900.
• S.A. Swedish postcard, circa 1930.
• Gertrud Caspari. *Lustiges Kleinkinderbüch*. circa 1910.
• Anonymous. German postcard. circa 1910.
• Clara E. Atwood. *Field and Tree*. 1923.
• Honor C. Appleton. *Songs of Innocence*. circa 1911.
• Anonymous. *Chatterbox*. 1899.
• W. Heath Robinson. "A Christmas Deed of Kindness." circa 1932.
• Henry Ford. *The Orange Fairy Book*. 1903.
• Florence & Margaret Hoopes. *Good Times*. 1932.
• Lorentz Frœlich. *Bonsoir Petit Père*. circa 1873.
• M. Ellen Edwards. *Told in the Twilight*. circa 1890.
• Robert Barnes. *Storyland*. circa 1885.
• Jessie Willcox Smith. *At The Back of the North Wind*. 1919.
• Anonymous. *Chatterbox*. 1874.
• Lizzie Mack. *Old Father Santa Claus*. circa 1885.
• E. Hatton Stanton. *Father Tuck's Annual*. circa 1905.
Back Cover
• John D. Batten. *Indian Fairy Tales*. 1892.